Mario Pet

somewhere is january

selected from *i tulips*
by Peter Brennan

PERDIKA EDITIONS 7

PERDIKA EDITIONS 7
Series Editors: Peter Brennan,
Mario Petrucci & Nicholas Potamitis

Published by Perdika Press
2007

Perdika Press
16B St. Andrew's Road
Enfield MIDDX
EN1 3UB UK

www.perdikapress.com

Set by N. Potamitis in Monotype Joanna

ISBN: 978-1-905649-06-8

Acknowledgements

Some of these poems appear in *Envoi*.

My gratitude to Brennos and Agnetta for their constant,
constructive attention, and for supplying, often, a
fascinatingly bipolar response. I am especially indebted to
Peter, who has answered my request for a Perdikan
perspective on the (still spreading) *i tulips* sequence by
finding in it what Frank O'Hara called "the sea at the back of
my eyes, near the spot where I think".

"The whole of the music could be in these tunings."

Robert Duncan

SPRING

Our cells reply as petals do —
beflowering the nervous
byways. Gusts shake

temporal memories
loose: bestrew a mind's
street corners. If hail should

pass — it will thaw quickly as
we do. This blood tight in
its arteries second by

second taking us
to heart may be loosed
in that simple space between

two beats of thought. Nothing
lost. Spring prepares
that tender and

final passage —
gathers us (soft tendrils
that we are) back to the root.

for Denise Levertov

tulip

repeats as
if it were me
-rely one pouring

upwards to melt
light with
light

: others
doing same
shake loose this

pane squaring on
to one square
field of

them
as sun turns
up its yellow dial

& volumed glow
eases petals
apart

as many
-petalled pelvis
is eased by red birth

or womb could
split & leave
its black

& yellow
baby standing
alert – ready almost

to speak

no light except

what dark makes room
for – cosmos a jostle
jowl to shoulder of

suns that burn c-
old & near-empty to
birth out dark between th-

in thighs of constellations
& what gas this flesh
must be to fill

wastes with or
thread each hurled
wire of photon – till

self-erect with these
hot eyes i ablate
light in near-

black swathes of
absence even as it s-
urges back remembered &

renewed

days when sun

dips white &
simple between two
brick-hard places across

the way – framed by lace
trees & streaking desk
with chalk – then

dimming to its
last flare inspires dust-
lazy eddies in which i see my

maiden form as house all at
once swivels to a crystal
of beam & plaster

to catch brief
gleam of silence & if
i could i would take that

thin wrist of dust – fix my
grip on it & lead me
out of the light

solace is never

too late: always that sun
tears cloud from c-
loud like child

left with paper
whose light little
hands turn sheet to

deckle – a making of
edges thinner thus
whiter with

brighter linings:
those eeled edgings
electric with light where

eye rests – can acknowledge
there the grey within:
each shifting

billow of word
too few – a word too
curt – like sun dimmed

behind a white it brings
more white to *just* as
warmth is required

for bloom to
feel requited &
without strain make

an opening – yet
still to cloud-
burst dark

she opens

i rather love

not things but
what lies behind
these the way a year

is sometimes glimpsed
past ear of corn or
december

come
out of blue to
one who knew only

sun – perhaps such
are best unsaid
so all might

speak of
corn & sky or
strip decembers

down to black-
scaffold
trees

where
life sings &
sings to death each

silenced thing

i went t-

here where few
have been though
most have trampled

it in thought – easy to
say that name we
give it or what

one means by
it or where when
waves of a hand can

get to it faster than
light: but i think
i have been

there
if just for
one thought & if

once then one never
quite comes back
– or did i let

loose each th-
ought of me to rise
& spread as steam th-

inking that an edge or very
heat of possibility
when really

all that
happened had
already happened & i

simply fell as all
do but felt it
in me

in many pl-
aces at once as
rain is

i court this

kinship with
late-showering
evening – frosted

pane half open brings
two cousins of
vapour : one

up nape of
west blushing to
fragile pate : the other

here – spating my core
as if i were its
filament

its rate
of heat &
now an other form

·within : water not as
gas or crystal
nor liquid

quite –
but percolating
pores of dilating earth

made upright & walking
its fourth estate   so
let coition

wait – that
soft-thrusting con
-undrum of dissolution

wait – for now swimming
is agate square of
me slopping

its edges
& bathing returns
this freight snug to mould

that cast me   & tucked
in behind you
sated by

dark (even
when you hold my
breath) is not mating or love

only – but a fresh
state plain as i
-ce prior to

the skate
: a spooning force
new-discovered – this

shuddering natal cosmos
drawing almost too
late like

to like

there is more to

this morning than blades
transfigured by frost –
its needling army

of unbending
spear-bearing christs –
more than that lowish ruddy

madonna waking from being
too long in the east
glancing in to

clear her throat
through brightening
range of orange & scissor

from a black-green field
fringed by poplars her
moon-doily of un-

defrosted shadows
as though the land were
her single child made many

-faced & already old by
excess tutelage in
whose orders

whirring space
seeks this young-hunched
form of light or grinding through

layered dogmas of physics
hopes to put all in its
simple place only

to receive un-
knowing the one
devotee who stays &

stays even as mother becomes
unconscious with rising
& shadows fall

to their knees

for Robert Creeley

sea   take

off that cloak —
wide dark
against

darker
sky — come
to love   love

more sound
than light
though

soon
from bed
lover shall rise

to join us — that
holy head
a coin

sullen
with love —
then night & in-

coming locks
will whiten
with time

till i
am one
who leaves

her in white to
look out on
sand

&

(i turn
this back
to sleep)   ah

how i must
sleep to
dream

       sea

that it was there

neither of us would
doubt – but a kind
easily lived

without – which is to
say unembroidered
by flame & un-

pressured by heat – the
same way certain
words one

grows into flailing some
times fall cool with
own weight &

sleek as tails into long-lined
rhyme – ours was
plain

as sand achieved grain by g–
rain to aggregate
its whitened

beach where shells or men of
war might wash up
clean of

blood as two long-drifting
hearts should (each
one saved by

the other shore) rocking
hairily buoyant &
warmed as

milk sun dropped to
ferment this
inner

fizz i raise to you
across blue
time

then drink to
love that
is

when you see

the scale of it −
    not
near-up as one-

shaded bough or
    half
-garden sliced thru

by its sundialling h-
    our
but   laid out   a wr-

inkling of what goes
    deeper
than substance you

walk on   bulked to
    shift
& curvature & as gr-

avid belly veined d-
    ark
by waters shown up

as planetary   cause i
    have
gone further from it:

no choice nor circum-
    stance
but   detail   hand in

mouth with turning &
    never
happening   but very

    ground

sanctuary of

APHAIA – not only fluted
pillar but this
clutched

pink
in its crevice
with blood in the throat –

not the felled bolus against
headaches of gods
but

slumbering
woman-child feeling
stone through her back   not

booth   not caption   nor
flies rubbing hands
but

gaze
so patient these
foundations pull loose &

warp

for when these eyes

are yours at last & yours
mine – so neither
again depends

on way of facing
or putting something
on tables is done for who

happens to be sitting – or
one in-breathing is
another expiring

with shout of
beginnings & kiss of
ending – till then you &

i may look to star faint with
edge of seeing &
imagine

there
touched by all
worlds our world a

child sleeping

night draws in & a few

notes shared
with friend who sits by
lover & planes

furrow white
that nightling blue that
seems twilit

from behind
as fire goes white with
ash & moths

take air – so
we share a few notes as
dark rustles its

end-of-garden
skirts & last wine is br-
ought out till

none can tell
friend from lover or night
from these few

notes which
drift & rise through us &
out to hum with

dark above &
below so even the planes
pause in their

rough music

somewhere is january

all *else* – infatuate
in itself as downpouring
light air-shimmered or wrap of

body-heat against sleep or
non-sleep deep as
tilting planet as

here i re-
sort to combing
grass flattened in wind for

meaning & those first few
spots of words whose
hope i am whose

pearly colds
form laces to strang
-ulate till those hills of

face my mirror returns me
deepen their shade &
i seek refuge a

nebbish among
this race of children
believing sleigh for hearse

                    & i can do
nothing but remind
of winter

& go out with
no terms to meet rain
daggering ice with each

drop on my back &
bend my back
to it as i

walk this
self towards that
stick i made for it &

must one day walk-with
as if it were still
autumn

though
all is not gold
when around me &

topping me is white that
close-furrowed
white &

grey

the night the world

ended
they counted up –

found
one word too

many